WALKING HOME

BY

Michael D. Grover

Roadside Press

copyright

Editor: Michele McDannold

Roadside Press
Meredosia, Illinois

Contents

Walking Away From Cancer

Walking away from cancer
As long as this journey has been
There is a lot of inertia
Walking away from death
It is a slow process
It is a slow crawl
Patience has been worn
& it's too fucking easy
Just to lay down in the recliner
In front of the tv & die there
Who would blame you if you did
This journey is hard
& requires the will to live

Walking Away From Cancer #2

Walking away from cancer

I try to keep moving forward

Not back to where I've been

I follow my intuition

I walk the dog everyday

When it starts to get comfortable

I push farther

Right now I'm up to two miles

The dog sees other dogs along the way

He tugs at the leash to go back to see them

I jerk it forward

Walking Away From Cancer #3

Walking away from cancer
                    from the edge of death
It's like walking into the unknown
You don't know what you'll be when you get there

Walking Away From A Super Blood Flower Moon

Walking away from a super blood flower moon

I just have to keep my shit together

It's hard to keep steering forward

When there is a bend in the road

And you don't know what you're heading into

Walking Away From The Last Time I Played Jazz

I am playing Jazz
It is the first time in a long time
I feel I should make it a morning ritual

It feels like 2017, it is December in Toledo, Ohio
Outside it is fifteen below
Everything covered in a two-foot blanket of static snow
Inside, warm light shined
Wild Jazz played day & night

Today heat, humidity, Florida Summer thunderstorms
I am listening to Jazz & writing
It has come full circle

Walking Away From Fear

Walking away from those things
You have witnessed
You have seen with your eyes
That society deems conspiracy

The same way your country needs you working
To pay off that debt that they keep raising
To make some other man rich
Your country needs you to consume
To keep up with your neighbors
But they are experienced and quite cruel
In the art of poverty
Please sit back, relax, support the advertisers

Walking Away From What I Used To Be

I am trying to tell you
I don't even know who I am talking to
This is a transmission to the future
What I have to say
Is if I walk out of this alive
I don't know what I'm going to be
Will I be that ghost writer
Just blending into the background
If I walk away from cancer
I would say cancer is like
Moving at fourth dimension speed
In case you didn't know it's slower
I am trying to get back to the third
Not fade away like a ghost

Walking Away From Poetry

(For Wayne Mason)

I am reading a book by a Poet

How he works in a meditative state

Repetitive robot factory motion

He says he's become invisible

He says he's walked away

I think about the craft

The more we develop our style

The more isolated & invisible we become

We blend in with the background noise

We blend in to bear witness

And we wonder why nobody sees us

Walking Away From Trauma

(For Greg Clean)

I've seen violence on the battlefield
Violence done by a system so cruel
Protesters on the front line,
Ordinary people given a different vision
Had to turn to drugs, & alcohol
Homeless shelter to cheap weekly motel

Like a veteran, I carry these visions around
Dying like dogs in the street
His sister took all of his Poetry
She probably burned it first chance she got

Like a veteran, I carry these scars around
If I went to Wesley's, he'd buy me beers all night
He had come into a disability settlement
Everyone loved him, he'd been buying them beers all day
Either of us knew, we both had liver cancer
This would be my last impression of him
Happy & on top of the World

I don't want to remember that last time
In the hospice, in a coma, a bliss like grin
You died three hours after we left

I have seen things on the battlefield
That I cannot unsee

Walking Away From Space

We all look to space
Way up high in the sky
We strain our necks
Staring into space
Some perfect projection
Atop a prison planet

I'm going to tell you something
That they don't want you to know
Space is on the inside
It is there for you to explore
This entire unknown realm
You don't even have to leave the back yard

Yeah, space is the place
They don't want you to know it's out there
We may connect with our potential,
Our real selves

Walking Away From Memory

It's a funny thing
It visits me like ghosts
Trauma from the past into now
Things that serve no purpose
Then I can't remember a fucking password
Memory can be a funny thing

Walking Away From Myself

Do I know who I am anymore
Or do I know myself too well
Creature of instinct
                    impulse
I am the birds outside
The birds are me
I am the visions that I see
Sounds that I hear
They are me
Everything here at this moment
For some perfect reason
We're just out here
Waiting for a sign
Waiting on the phone
Waiting in a waiting room
Waiting for the doctor
Waiting for paperwork
Waiting . . .
All there is left to do
Writing pyramids on the page

What kind of grid could that be

What kind of intention

Talking to stones

Fading into the background

Recovery is a bitch

Waiting . . .

Knowing time is short

Stretching time

Waiting . . .

Walking Away From Memory #2

Is a bitch
I have memories
I can't remember what I was before this
Or how I got there
How in the end
I was just hanging on a lifeboat
If I make it out of this
I will never be the same again
I don't know if there's a place for
What I've become
That's the fear that keeps holding me back
Fear of starting over
Pushing farther outward/inward
I can't see a clear path
To what I am becoming
Walking in darkness for so long
Will I be able to survive out there
Every day I walk through darkness
Every day I grow stronger

Those voices in my head keep whispering to me

This is the right direction

We are aligned

Walking Away From Memory #3

I feel like the great smudge stick of time

Has passed over me

& I inhaled its sweet smoke

I feel like my mind got reset

& I don't know who I am

I only know what I am becoming

I walked down the street to a shop today

It felt strange & alien to me

I felt so free

Walking Away From The Future

Watching Sunday morning television evangelist
While the tv is muted
Crazy Jazz filling the room
He looks like a stand-up comic or a clown
Saying nothing funny
Dancing around, waving his arms like a chicken
So desperate for the camera's attention

The madness it purifies you
It strips you of everything
Shedding skin like a snake
Preservation to stay alive
Survive things that inevitably will come
You build shrines of protection all around you
You build those walls as high as you can
Knowing they will never be high enough
To protect you from what's coming

Walking Away From Darkness

There is light in darkness
Don't let anyone tell you different
Some see black as the absence of color
Some see black as a combination of color
This darkness that is coming
It is all encompassing
It will take over everything

I want you to know if you read this
That you make your own light
& you had better get used to using it
Because darkness is upon us
Maybe you didn't see it sneak into the room
Maybe you can't see it because it's been there all along
Blending into the background like a chameleon

They hate the light
So they will come for you
Keep yourself well protected

Make yourself invisible
Fade into the background like they do

This war has been going on for centuries
Shall we go through the list
Of martyrs martyred for Poetic visions
It's a World-wide tradition

The television can spout a million truths
For millions of different people
But it's never gonna tell the truth
The truth is it would upset the advertisers
It's the truth verses a lie
It's always going, repeating

We are the inertia to the war machine
Always grinding it down
Always have, and always will be
And the story goes on
We all know in the end the Poet dies on the losing side
But in the end
The Poet dies with a smile on their face

Knowing there is light in darkness

We create our own light

Now, be the light

Shine as bright as you can

Amplify it, let them know

Walking Away From The Light

Shine your light in darkness
Shine your light
Because the darkness is upon us
Just because the news never reported it
Does that mean it didn't happen
Like a tree that fell in the forest
Will no one hear
Do they control the narrative
Or do you believe what you see
Because everybody's talkin' real loud
But nobody's saying a thing

When you were so young, you could see them
They would tell you terrible things
Nurture you in your nightmares
So long ago you can't remember
But the fear still lives
    the fear they planted

You control the narrative

You the great storyteller

You hold the light

They fear the light

Be the light

They will try to suck the oxygen out of the air

As not to feed that fire inside you

Let it glow

Walking Away From Corporate Programming

Watching the new corporate programming

You pick the side or fascist

You follow into servitude

They control the narrative

The right and left brains

Make sure they hate each other

So they may never get together

And get the story straight

Create a void of fear & hate so dark

No light can escape through

Weaponize politics

Then give the order to attack

In the end we're all the same

We bleed the same red blood

In the end the fear and hate

Lies heavy in the air like the humidity

It's all just food for them

They must be hungry

Walking Away From Magic

Most people today would walk away from magical things
Like a sunrise at Stonehenge perfectly aligned
A picture heard around the World vibrating
It's too easy to turn away
To say it was the camera angle
And return to the noise of the tv
They'll believe anything it says
Not mystical things like Poetry
Not real things you can see
Not things hiding in shadows
Things they don't want you to see
Things they don't want you to believe

Walking Away From Cruel Gods

God feeds on negative emotions
That's why they put so much fear,

                         stress,

                         violence

On the tv
They don't want you to know
The fact is we're all like batteries in the matrix
We are all so easily programed
We are all here to serve our
Masters, creators, gods

Walking Away From Darkness #2

Poets we are messengers of the dark
Constantly shifting our minds to different realities
So we may create in the dark
Dwellers and seers of other dimensions
Just to catch a few lines, the next Poem

Now we watch the darkness descend on everyone
Spreading like a virus
We know this darkness as a necessary evil
Poets don't fear the darkness
Show them the way
Show them the light

Walking Away From The Lizard Queen

There is a giant talking lizard on the tv selling insurance

The queen is dead

Jonny Rotten smiles in his grave

Walking Away From The Shitstorm

(For Drew Coomer)

People losing touch
In this shitstorm life
Who could blame them for not answering a text
They're out trying to save the World
Or themselves from it

Feels like I've been standing here, stagnant
Slow crawl to the unknown
I'm no psychic, can't see the future
No clue what I've been walking into
Can't remember what I used to be
All that I know is it isn't good

Online there is a race of starving artists
Looking to eat the few crumbs america left scattered around
All I know is no one is going anywhere here
Because we all end up in the same place in the end
All I know is that I really miss human interaction
Feeling connected to something, anything

The other day an old friend came to visit

I felt like they all had forgotten me

It was like real human contact

People losing touch

In this shitstorm life

Walking Away From The Border

I was born in a border town

West Palm Beach, Florida

Only the border was made of ocean

Sometimes they would wash up on the shore

What is legal

Who is illegal

What's the difference

Money

Is this what the World revolves around

Money

What is fueling the republican party

Money

What is fueling the democratic party

Money

The republican party is terrified of the truth

So they whitewash all impurities away

The democratic party is terrified of the truth

That's why they fear Bernie Sanders

The media is terrified of the truth

Because they sell PR to the oppressors

So they may oppress more

It's where the money is

A moment of silence

Compassion for those who stop to feel

Those who feel alone in isolation

There are real human lives on the board

Real human lives promised a paradise

Used as a pawn in some rich white governor's political message

Everyone talking about eliminating the enemy

Well the enemy is the one doing the talking

We are just listening

Waiting for a better day

A day when opinions are not fed through a flat screen

I listen to hear the motives behind it

Walking Away From Summer

I am not important
I am just a cog
The queen was not bigger
Than anyone I know
No one is bigger
Than the whole of us
Not just the human whole
But the whole damn thing

It is mid-September in Florida
It is a cool morning so I sit outside
Listening to birds, lawnmowers, and chainsaws
The only place to get away
From TV noise
So I stimulate the mind with Sexton & McClure

Walking Away From The Beast Of Compassion

The beast of compassion speaks

Words come, no action

A multi-cultural rainbow of peacock feathers

All the same color, green

Some intergalactic turf war

Powers that are higher than we could comprehend

To control the Earth and its resources

For those who are a pawn in this game, change the game

Walking Away From Ourselves

Forgive me,

We are all gods with fragile egos

Walking away from what we were

Walking Away From Ian

If you survive the storm
america has no compassion
Leave you to die in the street like a dog
Fighting for food, fighting for gasoline
My dog snoring in a bed
As I write by candle light

Walking Away From america

america, I am fifty-four years old
& I've never known freedom
I have been told I had it all of my life
But freedom is elusive

Freedom to write a Poem
I have read female Poets rant about freedom
Ms. DiPrima and Smith
And how it's so elusive
I've read the directions
By d.a. levy himself
I've worshipped at his grave
Looking for freedom

Truth is I had it all along
america, I almost died
I don't understand what's walking away from that
But it's a being of high energy
That is making a lot of positive progress
But I've still got a long way to go

america, when I make it there

I don't know what my place will be

america, I am scared that I won't be able to afford

This freedom that you advertise

Like it was just a buzz word republicans throw around

Because most people are too stupid to vote

america, I have a confession

I was born working middle class

My father was a socialist union electrician

Maybe I was conditioned a little different from most

I tried so hard to walk in his shoes

It was easy to skate by my dad was the foreman

And I'd have one of his best friends as a journeyman

One day the shop Stuart got ahold of me

*Mike this isn't really for you, you had better stick to that
writing that you do*

I was learning things, but we all knew I was just skating by

So when the job ended I was out of the apprenticeship

But does Glen Lucky know that writing doesn't pay

america, I don't have the freedom to avoid a major hurricane
But you're letting the oil lobby speak for you again

america, my father doesn't speak to me anymore
What am I supposed to do america
I'm guessing that he's disappointed in my choice
As to what I can become
He always told me I could be anything I wanted to be

america, we can't all be cookie cutter corporate
Where's the freedom to be different
Ask any politician you'll hear a bunch of buzz words coming out
Words that used to mean something, words like freedom
Words republicans now get paid not to say like climate change

Or just these moments where we sit here alone writing a Poem
Freedom is elusive

Walking Away From The Clock

I want and need some resistance

Not a perfect cookie cutter World

Where everyone loves the lie the country stands
for

& truth would be treason

& we all believe in the war machine

Because they keep us free

To buy what we can afford to buy

Big brother watching back through screen to
screen to screen

All seeing eye on street

From the heavens if necessary

Watching from phone right by your side

Not just watching, listening

All seeing eye sees too much

Maybe time to move the hands counter clock-
wise

Deploy a little chaos into the mix

Follow your intuition

Walking Away With Visions

Walking away with the visions that you've seen
They were only meant for you

Walking Away From Opinion

Opinion, political or religious belief

To rain yours down

Like the voice of god

Like a bully pulpit

To think apart from the mob of popular opinion

& be free to express your own thoughts

Not the recycled opinions of others

Walking Away From Recovery

Sit in the middle of this chaos

This healing process

Life goes on

Navigating through

Manifesting luck and prosperity

Weight grows heavy

It was meant to go this way

Forward . . . into the unknown

Eating fear of the future as we go

Setting the past on fire

The ghost ship leaves a trail to my door

Walking Away From Poetry #2

Poetry I have lived my life
Following you to your logical end
Here I am at fifty-four
I have cancer, and live with my mother
How's that for an american dream

Poetry we have concluded
There is no mass Poet conciseness
There are cool guys, and not so cool
Like high school all over again
Nobody gives a shit about any of it

Poetry you have drug me through the streets
Of the Bottom of West Philly
Through the dirty streets of East Hollywood
There has never been a place that didn't feel like home
But what was it all for Poetry
To suffer like this
To write from memory from afar
About distant places I used to know

To have cancer in a pandemic
Where the virus could kill me

Poetry my father doesn't have caller ID
He just hangs up when it's me
This has progressed from sighing
Like something bothered him
Over and over when I called

Poetry I have lived my life
Following you to your logical end
Obviously we're not quite there yet

Walking Away From Language

Did I cut myself with Poetry

Only to bleed on the floor

Of small apartments all of those years

Perfect Worlds of chaos and magic

Perfect World to conjure some words

Always inside words matter

Always a screen a window to the outside

Where language gets manipulated and butchered

Like the governor who tells the state

They voted to stay free

When there are no abortions

You can't tell his bratty spoiled kids

The truth that they live on stolen land

So freedom is just a word to him

Out of his mouth a dirty word

Soon they will come for the separation of church & state

As this freedom spreads

We must preserve the language

Walking Away From The Lizard

There is something so engrained
So deep in all of us
It is part of our brain
              Our dna
It is right there
At the base of the spine
Waiting to uncoil and strike

They are cruel gods to us
              creators,
              artists,
              architects,

They are all around us
Just beyond the peripheral vision

Let yours loose inside
Control it, don't allow it to control you

Walking Away From Los Angeles

I smile as I think back to simpler times

When words I wrote down on the page with real ink

The only thing that could be permanent in LA

Day after day grinding in a telemarketing office

Until my head hurt

I could watch the sunset on the hills from the fire escape

& melt it away with words

Walking Away From The Invisible Poet

For his last act he will continue
To disappear from this plane
To fade into the background
Like he was never here
Pen in hand grinding at the pulp of trees
No body notices or much cares
What could be better than self
A whole World of things
Nobody hears, muffled by the facebook cries for relevancy
Kissing the ass of false idols, mediocre Sages and Seers
Who just love too much to get their ass kissed
And looks down on the kissers

Some of us are different
We infest the landscape like aliens
We only want to be ourselves
We're not here for fame or money
We only want respect
And there is no respect or dignity in writing
We only want to be ourselves

Our true selves

Bigger than ourselves

america does not honor creation

Only destruction

So we must tear each other down

To reach for a singular prize, that's not there

Nobody cares

Stop, it's not for me

We are dying inside from fighting all our lives

Bodies full of bad energy

We cannot see the light because we are the fucking light

The farther we walk into darkness

The darker it seems

I have been there

I have walked into the darkness

& it has changed me

Now that I see the light again I am walking into it

I don't know what I am anymore

But I'm learning as I keep walking

I am walking forward invisible no more

How long can I last in a World where the truth is treason

Ask Ezra Pound that

You'd better ask d.a. levy

Ask fucking Lorca or Neruda

You'd better ask yourself just how far you're willing to take this

Walking Away From Trauma

It comes like a blow

        an impact

Turning all of your energy

To negative pushing you lower than low

You remember everything you couldn't be

How your father won't even talk to trash to you anymore

How you wish that you could tell your father

That you like him better silent

Because he talks far too loud

& he says things that parents should never say to their children

It hits too hard

It cripples me

It reminds me that I'm not complete

Maybe I am the failure they say I am

But the truth is I have never lived by their standards

I build myself better in my own way

Walking Away From Intellectuals

What will you say

When asked what you did to stop it

Teaching from your Ivory Towers

To a bunch of protected rich kids

Who will never know the coldness or hardness

Of concepts such as poverty

& why preach against a system

That has done so well for you

Walking Away From america's Pick Your Reality

You can choose to see a prison
That is what you shall see
If we see a nation where hard work is rewarded
Then we had better get to work
Perception is reality
America is what you see
Medea has news and lies
To pile up on every side
No individual thinking, no independent thought
It will be interrupted by noise of commercials
To shut down intellectual functions
Watch the violence, fill with fear
Our cruel gods they feed on that
We are like food or batteries
They are all hungry
Remember, perception is reality
It doesn't matter how you make it
Remember that you are reality

Walking Away From The american Artist

He woke up in a strange World of conformity

Though he always pushed resistance

A World that he'd been exiled from

Exiled from his country for free thought

He tried to save the people

Who were lock step marching

To the master's trumpet

They did not want to be saved

There was nothing wrong with them

In fact there was something wrong with him

He was woke not sleep

To the soothing sound of the master's trumpet

The commercials say jesus was no savage lizard after all

He was one of us

Paid for by lizards

There was something wrong

Walking Away From The Poem

(For Denise Levertov)

The Poem comes down

From the sky somewhere

Maybe inside the head

Part of the great expanse/void

Healing Poems of natural flow

Flowing through the conduit

Healing Poems cleansing body & soul

Poems hated by the powerful

Because the Poem said *You've got the power*

Poems that liberated

Poems hated by oppressors of mind and soul

Poems passed down to me

By Levertov and other greats

Poems that never got heard enough

Because they had something to say

Poems that tell truth

As government & powers of Poetry deny

Walking Away From Greed

Strange days as the hawk flies by

Change is in the wind like angel's breath

The future is a lighter place

We're gonna walk away from the darkness

This darkness that we surround ourselves with

This shame that we carry

So we can't shine our beauty to the World

Till we can't see the beauty of the World

You go with the flow take what you need

Leave things for others walk away from greed

Walking Away From The Pause

It's all about the pause
The time between things
The time that you are aware, listening
Writing things down
That time between reading another manuscript,
And starting my sacred daily ritual of meditation
Magic comes, ideas come, words come
It's all about the pause

Walking Away From Gunfire

Sunday morning Sabbath
Filled with Poetry & meditation
Interrupted by automatic weapon fire
Slicing through the calm air
Someone might have gotten gunned down
Right in these country streets
Where the birds sing from the trees
And the rooster crows

The truth is it's not an uncommon sound around here
It's the sound of freedom
It's the sound of some good old boy
Popping off a few rounds in the backyard
Preparing for the next uncivil war
That never comes, but they're ready

Walking Away From Ego

Sometimes all we can hear is the negativity

All that we want is conflict

We can't see of hear the praise right in front of us

This is the ego talking

The great negative vibe

We must raise our vibration

High enough to hear it

Higher than disease that infests the body

Walking Away From Gatekeepers

When the gatekeepers come
Art becomes less about meaning
    becomes less threatening
A mean dog with no teeth
Constantly barking all of the time
Never saying or doing anything
Complacent of its imaginary ground
Like a corrupt politician
That everyone trusts but they never see

Walking Away From Lerner

Waking up is hard

Realizing the World is just

Illusion on top of illusion

News is the corporate illusion

So they don't offend the advertisers

Few see the whole World

I've been working so hard

So I can manifest a reality just creating

Where I don't spend the best years

Of my life destroying my body

Things are different now

Our lives work journaled

What was it all for

It had to be bigger than this

Walking Away From Magic #2

We find new Worlds
Of hope and possibility
Buried inside of the same old one
And we wonder what else they might have buried here

Walking Away From Gunfire #2

Muffled thunder of distant gunfire

Like a warzone

In this peaceful Southern town

Where birds sing, and squirrels play

Where the wind blows

Where the flag flies

Where the Sabbath is

Where Neruda is

Where the peace is

It breaks it

Walking Away From The Bullying Voices Of america

They will haunt you

They will scream at you

They will say: Why do you have to be you

After all this is america

And you can be anything you want

So dream big, and shoot low

And maybe you can be not what you are

But what could you be

You could be an image, product, brand,

You could be a star, and talk loud & important on the tv"

And what I say to the bullying voices of america is "Fuck you"

We are bigger than our egos

We shine brighter than a thousand healing suns

We shine in your darkness america

The darkness of the fear of your prison in tow from sea to shining sea

The fear of your culture wars and the cross and the flag

The fear of different being erased

Fear of book bans, fear of ignorance

Fear of the Dragon, the unseen hand

You can keep it all america

It's that fear that fuels you

It's that fear that is in control

I refuse to accept this reality,

I refuse to accept this negativity

Over the years Michael D. Grover has become a legendary underground Poet. Back in the early 2000s he ran Covert Press and worked with many of the giants of underground Poetry. Over the years Michael has been published in countless publications all over the World, and published over fifteen books of Poetry. Michael spent over ten years as head Poetry editor of the literary zine *Red Fez*. Michael has published two novels. Michael currently lives in Florida, dealing with cancer, with his dog where he meditates every day.

MORE ROADSIDE PRESS TITLES:

By Plane, Train or Coincidence
Michele McDannold

Prying
Jack Micheline, Charles Bukowski and Catfish
McDaris

Wolf Whistles Behind the Dumpster
Dan Provost

*Busking Blues: Recollections of a Chicago Street
Musician and Squatter*
Westley Heine

Unknowable Things
Kerry Trautman

How to Play House
Heather Dorn

Kiss the Heathens
Ryan Quinn Flanagan

St. James Infirmary
Steven Meloan

Street Corner Spirits
Westley Heine

A Room Above a Convenience Store
William Taylor Jr.

Resurrection Song
George Wallace

MORE ROADSIDE PRESS TITLES:

Nothing and Too Much to Talk About
Nancy Patrice Davenport

Bar Guide for the Seriously Deranged
Alan Catlin

Born on Good Friday
Nathan Graziano

Under Normal Conditions
Karl Koweski

The Dead and the Desperate
Dan Denton

Clown Gravy
Misti Rainwater-Lites

Milton Keynes UK
Ingram Content Group UK Ltd.
UKHW010937221123
433051UK00001B/22